All the buildings in the foreground of this picture of Townhead have been demolished, and the whole area is now occupied by housing for senior citizens. The three storey building on the right hand side was once the Masonic Hall Lodge St John No. 39. In later years the lodge moved to Parkfoot Street. The ground floor of the building was then used as dwellinghouses and the middle and top floor was bought by the Orange Lodge. At the start of the century an old Presbyterian minister occasionally used the hall as a venue for educating children of both religions, but the venture was short-lived. During this period there was no Roman Catholic church in Kilsyth but a travelling priest from Campsie advised his parishioners to withdraw their children from the minister's classes. The building was demolished in the 1980s.

Murdoch & Company's coffin furniture factory was one of the main local works, providing employment for Kilsythians and people from the surrounding villages of Banton, Queenzieburn, Croy and Twechar. Its owner, Robert Murdoch, was a former provost of Kilsyth. His first factory was at Parkfoot Street, but he later moved to a new purpose-built factory at Innsbridge on the banks of the Garrell Burn. The company soon became the largest employer in Kilsyth and the only maker of coffin furniture in Scotland. In the picture men and women are hard at work in 'the rumble room' or 'big boiler'.

Old Kilsyth

by

William Chalmers

Lorries belonging to Alex Dunn outside Murdoch's factory, Innsbridge. Alex played an active part in the community, and during the building of Kilsyth Rangers' football pitch supplied lorries and drivers free of charge to ferry the pit waste which was used to level Duncansfield Park. His business was still in existence when Cumbernauld New Town was being built.

© William Chalmers 1997
First Published in the United Kingdom, 1997
by Stenlake Publishing Limited
01290 551122
www.stenlake.co.uk

ISBN 9781840336412

Printed by
Blissetts, Roslin Road, Acton, W3 8DH

Miller's Dam. The dammed water once powered the old mill on the opposite side of Tak-Ma-Doon Road. The Garrell Burn runs along the valley to the right of the picture.

Work in the polishing shop required complete concentration and there was little time for chatter. Elsewhere in the factory the upper floor women were busy sewing shrouds, while others packed them ready for distribution. Under the joint managing directorship of Messrs Tom and Roy Murdoch the family extended their business interests as far as South Africa. However, the Kilsyth business gradually began to falter, mainly due to dwindling demand, while the centre of the coffin furniture industry, located in Birmingham, flourished. For a number of years the staff worked reduced hours until the factory finally closed and the machinery was whisked over the border. The premises were demolished and private houses now occupy the site. All that remains of the once flourishing business is a statue in Burngreen Park donated by the Murdoch family.

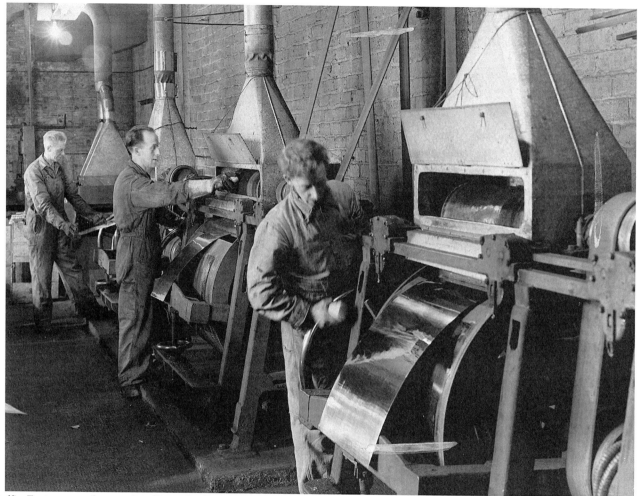

Murdoch's Coffin Factory was known locally as the Secret Works because of the clandestine government projects that it sometimes handled. Despite the secrecy, these jobs didn't tend to be very high security, and included making fittings for the Queen Mary. The man centre of picture, Sanny Brown, was one of the founders of Kilsyth Rangers after the First World War. On his return from the navy at the end of World War II he found that the team's overgrown pitch had been bought by the Roman Catholic Church as a sports field. The returning servicemen soon acquired a new plot of land called Duncan's field, ensuring the survival of one of Scotland's finest junior football teams.

Some of the young lads who worked at Murdoch's, probably photographed around the turn of the century. Included in the picture are: J. Miller, J. Chalmers, A Bankier, J. Rankin, J. Bamford, A. Motherwell, B. McFarlane, J. McCall, J. Primrose and his two brothers, B. Auld, Jack Provan, Tam Hutchison, J. Sneddon, J. Patrick, Jim Thomson and David Inglis.

The Stirlingshire Territorials 'A' Company, 7th Argyll and Sutherland Highlanders, at training camp, Montrose, 1928. Some of the men, in particular the senior NCOs, were survivors of the 1914 war; they are the ones wearing medals. The 7th went into action during the 1914-18 war with 31 officers, 1,100 NCOs and men. After little more than three weeks they were down to 2 officers – the Scott brothers from Tillicoultry – and 64 men. The incredibly heavy casualties were due to the German bombardment of their positions with gas. I only know the name of one of the soldiers in the picture, Sgt William Chalmers (my father), the first SNCO on the right.

The old Territorial building at the corner of Shuttle Street and Townhead. The drill hall, which was used during the Second World War by troops from Glasgow, the old HLI and later a battalion of Canadian soldiers who arrived in the United Kingdom for special hill and mountain training, stood to the rear of the property. A few of the Canadian soldiers married local girls and their families still live in Kilsyth.

Coal mining and quarrying became the main industries in Kilsyth when weaving went into decline during the early nineteenth century. Initially coal deposits near the surface were mined. Kilsyth Hills were rich in small but workable seams including those at Balcastle, Neilston, Highland Park, Riskend and Currymire. By 1860 the surface seams were all but worked out and shafts were being sunk at Currymire, Haugh, Craigends and Dumbreck. A hundred years of coal mining at Dumbreck Pit provided welcome employment for Kilsythians and the villagers of Queenzieburn, Banton, Twechar and Croy. But by the 1950s the pit was becoming uneconomical and its closure became inevitable. Today there is no trace of Dumbreck. The bings are gone and the whole area is now known as Dumbreck Marsh, a wildlife sanctuary.

The long sloping roofs of the miners' rows in this picture were coated in tar and the houses were jokingly known as the Torry Mansions. 'Hole-in-the-wall' beds in the kitchen usually supported three bed decks, often sleeping as many as ten people, while the small room at the back of the property was used by the parents and the youngest children. The outbuilding with the chimney and ventilation shaft was the wash-house. This contained an iron boiler which was fired with wood to bring water for washing clothes to the boil. The two and three storey buildings in the background were in Parkburn Road. Everything in the picture has been demolished.

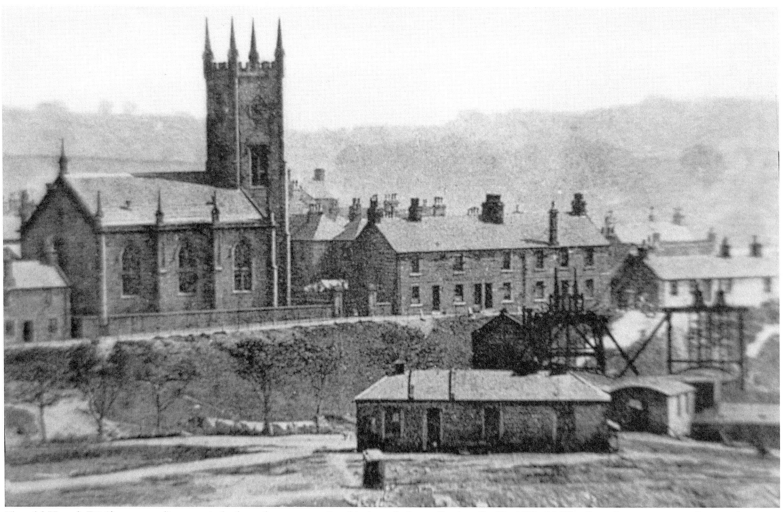

The old Haugh Pit (foreground) seems to be have been a very troubled workplace. During the First World War the mine owners cut the men's wages and warned them that they would sack them and employ ex-military men after the war if the new conditions were not accepted. The miners revolted and eventually the mine owners posted work notices in Ireland, offering men jobs in Scotland. This caused great hardship amongst the Kilsyth people. Local men returned to work under extreme duress, forced to accept the lower wages being paid to the immigrant workforce.

The houses in Backbrae Street (top left) have all been replaced with modern council flats. During the demolition of the Haugh Pit a young man was killed when part of the wall in the foreground fell on him. He was pulled clear but the attempts of Doctor Parker, whose surgery was across the Garrell Burn, could not save him. The Haugh Pit took the lives of many of the townsfolk. The old miners' footbridge is visible through the window of the partly demolished building.

West Burnside Street. One of the old miners' bridges, leading from the east side of Backbrae Street to West Burnside Street, is in the left foreground. The Garrell Burn (centre) begins high up in the Kilsyth Hills and starts its long journey down through the town from the Laird's Loup. The source of the burn is actually Johnny's Dam, just above the Birkin moor, although it only becomes the Garrell from Laird's Loup. The new Airdrie road occupies the site of the former miners' bridge, whilst all the buildings on West Burnside Street, including the gasworks, have been removed. A new housing development has recently got underway in the vicinity of the gasometers.

Engineers at Dumbreck Pithead, early 1950s. Top row, left to right, B. McConnell, Curry, Whyte, E. Wallace, H. Bradford, M. Patrick, Joe Sneddon, and J. Law. On 30 January 1938 nine miners lost their lives in the Dumbreck disaster, one of many tragic incidents that took place in the mines around Kilsyth and Twechar.

A turn of the century photograph taken at Kilsyth Kilns. The Haugh Pit stood to the rear of the kilns. Despite being Kilsythians, these men were employed at St Flannans Pit between Twechar and Kirkintilloch, and cycled to and from their work every day.

Kilsyth has always had a strong farming tradition. During the 1926 General Strike local farmers donated vegetables to soup kitchens which were set up in Kilsyth Academy playground in Shuttle Street. Harvesting time in October provided an opportunity for members of the local community to earn some much needed cash, and during the 1950s the education authorities allocated two or three school classes to help the farmers gather in their potato crop. The children were paid a small amount for each day's work and provided with lunch. The man with his hands full was a carter, and it was his job to lift the heavy wire baskets on to the cart. The women pickers were full-time farm helpers.

There is a long history of quarrying in Kilsyth and the surrounding villages. The earliest workings, the remains of which could be seen up until about thirty years ago, were situated slightly east of the stocking factory in an area known as the Blaeberryhill. When these became exhausted the main quarrying area was west of the town at Queenzieburn. Demand for whinstone was so great that more quarries came into production, including Auchinstarry (above), situated virtually on the banks of the Forth and Clyde Canal. Auchinstarry was worked up until the sixties and owned by Alexanders of Glasgow. The site has subsequently been landscaped by Cumbernauld and Kilsyth District Council, and now has picnicking, organised canoeing and rock climbing facilities.

Beltness Quarry, Kilsyth Hills. Top row, left to right: P. McAteer, A. Thomson, George Mitchell, W. Read, A. Thom, J. Hartley, J. Shields, D. Ross, D. McAllister, J. Thomson, M. Lowrie; front row, D. Abercrombie, K. Burns, W. Cree, J. Irvine, Wm. Shaw, unknown.

Old Mr Laing at Auchinstarry Quarry among his kerb stones, probably photographed around the turn of the century. Kilsyth, Queenzieburn, Banton, Banknock and Croy were all heavily involved in quarrying, supplying the city of Glasgow with whinstone, cobbles, kerbstones and bottoming for roads. After a spell as a soldier I got a job in Auchinstarry Quarry. I remember an old gentleman called Matt Derby from the village of Condorrat. 'Willie' he said, 'ye see that crow ower there – that's ma old workmate, who told me before he passed away "Matt, when ye see a crow sitting there you'll know its me. Whitever ye dae don't throw stanes at it fur it will be me back tae see how you're getting on"'. Not so many years ago I was working on a shrub bed which was sited where old Matt's binch (hut where the stone was dressed) had been. An eerie quiet came over the area and there was no one else within sight. A grey darkness prevailed, followed by a heavy snowfall, and a crow appeared in a tree above me . . .

The Wheasel Quarry, Kilsyth. Top row: Hope Comrie, J. McDonald (trainer, Kilsyth Rangers), W. Mathieson, M. Lowrie (of Banton), J. Abercrombie, Wm. Shaw, J. McKenzie, J. McGinnes. Second row: D. McAllister, W. Wilson, A. Easton, G. Douglas of Currymyre, unknown, W. Grant, G. Lowrie, A. Nichol, T. McGinnes, unknown, A. Thomson. Third row: Wm. Shaw sen., W. Mathieson sen., G. Shaw, the gaffer, Jimmy Shaw (of Banton; also known as deaf Jimmy), R. Abercrombie, W. Patrick, W. Pollock, unknown. Front row: B. Shaw, J. Taylor, W. Patrick (now in Australia), W. Ramsay, D. Abercrombie, G. Leishman, A. Thom, J. Mathieson. Early 1930s. These quarrymen were amongst the finest in the west of Scotland and with arms of steel dressed paving stones that were laid in Glasgow, Paisley and Edinburgh.

One of Alex Dunn's lorries leaving Murdoch's factory at Innsbridge, Kilsyth. Dunns ferried these crates to Glasgow docks from where they began their long sea journeys to parts of the Commonwealth as far afield as South Africa, Australia and Singapore.

Looking north along Kilsyth Main Street towards the Kelvinway housing scheme on Garrell Hill. The tenement block on the right was the old Co-op building and consisted of a dairy and footwear department with accommodation for employees above. Trains carrying coal used the bridge across Main Street to transport the black gold to Carron Ironworks. On the west side of the bridge, the line was used for commuter travel to Glasgow's Buchanan Street station. Today the bridge and most of the old buildings have gone. The flags and bunting were decorations for a May Day parade.

May Day parade, Main Street, 1950s. The boys and girls in the foreground have just crossed the footbridge over the Garrell Burn. This area of town was heavily picketed during the 1926 General Strike, and the marking of May Day was an extremely important event for miners and their families. A lot of the buildings in the picture have been replaced by less attractive modern structures. Main Street was recently dug up from top to bottom and resurfaced with cobbles imported from Europe. However there have been suggestions lately that a complete renovation of the street, could be on the cards again.

There was room for sixteen horses at Market Stables. Some of them were working horses and others could be hired with jaunting carts. There is nothing left of this building and in its place there is new housing for senior citizens. However they have kept one of the old names, the Cat's Close, at Market Square.

Thomson's boot and shoe repair shop in Westport Street, prior to its move to new premises in Market Street. The picture shows Jimmy Thomson and his young apprentice Robert Patrick who, as an officer with the Gordon Highlanders, was tragically killed near the end of the Second World War.

At some stage the furnishings from Dawson's Tearoom in Main Street were transferred to a shop in Glasgow, although unfortunately the whereabouts of this are not known. The present owner of the shop, David Cant, has recently had the interior upgraded, conserving some of the older fittings behind new building materials. In a hundred years time I am sure someone will appreciate the work. Dawson's Tearoom was an extremely important shop. The small hall was used for wedding receptions while the tearoom is probably best remembered by local shoppers who visited it on Saturday mornings. The pies and gravy were a particular favourite.

Kilsyth photographed from Parkfoot Street during the early 1900s. The building in the foreground was one of the town's many blacksmiths' shops. To the left is the old railway bridge crossing Main Street, with the former gas works beyond the railway line. At least ninety percent of the buildings in this picture have been demolished.

The Haggerty brothers in their yard at Parkfoot Street. Andrew is the man sitting in the cockpit of a flying flea an aircraft designed by Frenchman Henri Mignet. He also built a one man glider, an invention that the British military showed interest in. He is now in his eighties and the last time I saw him he was busy building a new sports car. The building in the background is Lodge St John No. 39, one of only a few old buildings left at the bottom of the town. The area where Andrew and his brother were photographed is now occupied by a games room and lounge adjoining the lodge.

This crime prevention bus was presented to Strathclyde Police by Kilsyth Rotary Club.

Kilsyth Police Station, Market Street, 1971.

Townhead Reservoir, known locally as the 'big dam', was formed by flooding the valley where the Battle of Kilsyth was fought. The reservoir is the main feeder for the Forth and Clyde Canal and has recently had the surrounding walls heightened to hold more water. This coincides with the recent announcement that the canal is to be upgraded using money from the Millennium Fund. The men in the picture, members of Kilsyth Fishing Club, are carrying fish stocks for releasing into the reservoir. The club had a reputation in virtually all Scotland's fishing waters and were renowned for their high catches. The man on the left is Mr Stark.

The fishing club on one of their many sorties on lochs and rivers outside Kilsyth. Rumour has it that when the Kilsyth club forewarned other areas that they would be fishing their waters on a particular day, their hosts would refuse them permission wherever possible. It was well known that the Kilsythians had a secret weapon, the minnow, which they used as bait.

Looking south-east from the Dummy Hill. The railway running through the town continued eastwards, passing the villages of Banton and Banknock towards Larbert. The same line was used at the outbreak of the First World War to carry the town's Argyll and Sutherland Highlanders on their journey to the battlefields of France. None of the houses in Parkfoot Street (foreground) have survived, and Kilsyth's first town council building now stands in the street. Initially there were plans for a swimming pool but Kilsythians considered this as the one that got away. Around seventy years later the townsfolk finally got the promised pool. Kelvinway, one of the new housing schemes to be built in Kilsyth in the early 1930s, stands just behind where this picture was taken from.

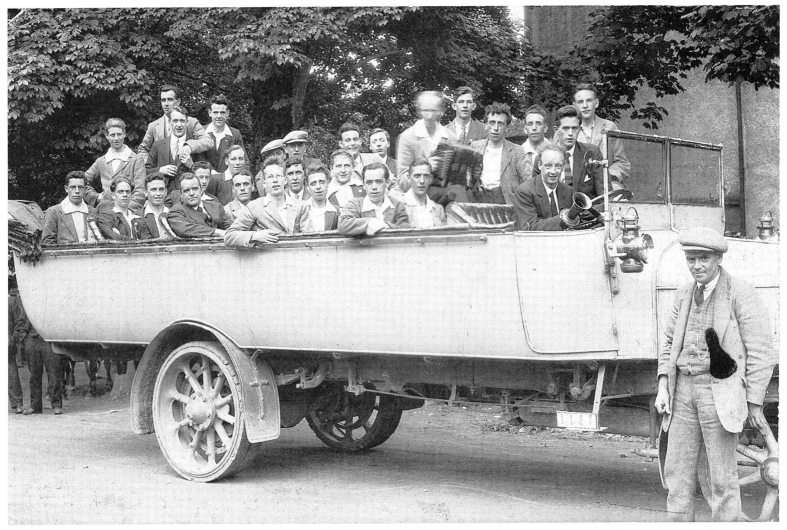

A group of bankers and young students on a day out. The bank trips were alternately run to the Ayrshire coast and Portobello on the Firth of Forth. Hard rubber wheels on this old charabanc couldn't have made for a very comfortable journey!

These houses were built to replace dilapidated sandstone buildings in the Backbrae, Church Street and Drumtrocher Street areas. With flat roofs they suffered from damp, and the unpopular houses became known locally as the Belsens. In later years they were upgraded, but it was felt by many of the inhabitants that they should have been demolished and replaced instead.

Members of the parks department at Colzium Lennox Estate, with a bedding display depicting the Kilsyth coat of arms. The men in the picture are, left to right, Robert Stevenson, J. McDonald, H. McCann, J. Nisbet, R. Anderson, D. Brown, J. Aitchison, W. Sim, J. Sneddon, and R. Allison. The estate was gifted to Kilsyth by the late lawyer William Lennox. It originally belonged to the Livingstons, an Episcopalian family whose allegiance with the Royalists during Scotland's civil war led to Sir William Livingston forfeiting his estates to the crown. Colzium House is situated on the site of the Livingston's castle.

Arnbrae House. In 1650, five years after the Battle of Kilsyth, Oliver Cromwell was on the rampage in Scotland. He burned down Kilsyth Castle, a revenge measure against Lord Kilsyth (who had supported the Royalist Montrose) and having fallen ill lay up in this house for the best part of a month while his Roundheads camped on the Kilsyth hillside. This important historical building has now been demolished.

An early photograph of Newtown Street showing thatched roofs and the old gas lamp standards. During the First and Second World War visiting troops used the street for drill practice.

Kilsyth Wanderers outside the Miners' Welfare Hall 1935-36. Top row: D. Binnie, W. Livingston, R. Whyte, E. Graham, J. McMillan, M. Stewart. Front row left to right J. Russell, V. Donnachie, J. Dubourdieu, A. Miller, J. Shaw.

Kilsyth Co-operative football team at the Miners' Welfare pitch near Burngreen. The pitch is still there, although it has been moved slightly to accommodate a new safety play area for children. Adjoining this is a model traffic scheme, where children can learn cycling proficiency skills. This was one of the first in Central Scotland and is regularly visited by groups from Glasgow and the surrounding areas. The pitch and adjoining land was purchased from the Scottish National Coal Board by Kilsyth Town Council around forty years ago and today there is a bowling green, a home for senior citizens, a health centre and a library there. Kilsythians can be proud of the fact that the town was the first in Stirlingshire to have its own library. Long before this was established, miners used to borrow books from a man named Mr Brash who lived near Charles Street. They would reputedly read the books standing under a gas-light, return them the same evening and call back the following night to complete them!

Duncansfield football ground, the location for this photograph, is home to Kilsyth Rangers Football Club. The team was disbanded at the outbreak of the Second World War and the servicemen returned to find that their Garrelvale football pitch had fallen into dereliction and been purchased by a local church. However they purchased a field from a local farmer, and after much hard work converted what was being used as a rubbish dump into one of Scotland's best junior grounds. The picture shows the NCB Scottish Miners team whose opponents on the day were the English NCB. The Scots beat their fellow miners 1 - 0. Top row, left to right: L. McFarlane, A. Lewesley, W. Woodside, J. Pollock, J. Shaw, D. Bailley, front row: S. Kennedy, J. Lochrie, J. Hartley, P. McLaren, J. Glover. Kneeling: A. Morris, transport manager Twechar yard. The men on either side were officials with the National Coal Board.

During the middle fifties Kilsyth Rangers won every cup in Central Scotland but the Scottish. They were an extremely competitive team and to play four or even five games in one week was not unheard of. The junior footballers of yesterday were paid in moderation and gave total commitment to their clubs and public. The man behind the wheel of the bus is Alex Binnie, once goalkeeper for Partick Thistle. I had the privilege to see documents from when Alex signed for one of the English first division teams – the fees were only a few pounds. Left to right: Alex Quarrie, centre forward Kilsyth Rangers, bus driver Jimmy McAulay, Rangers captain Willie Westwater (now in Australia), George Mulholl who later played for Aberdeen FC. Kneeling: A. Paterson, Rangers player and Neil Miller, former committee man and trainer.

This picture was taken at Burngreen, near the old Market House. The men in the picture were members of an organisation called the Shepherds which seems to have been run along the same lines as the Free Gardeners' Society. The wee boy at the front of the group is George Boyd of Queenzieburn, known locally as big Geordie Boyd.

The Turnpike Hall, now demolished, was used by a variety of organisations. During the 1926 strike the miners received two shillings and sixpence, money donated from the Russian Miners Union, which was distributed at the hall. At one time there was a Royal Navy Ordnance Depot at the corner of King Street. This was destroyed at the turn of the century by fire and probably stood in the foreground of this picture.

Three Kilsythians on a day run to the Brig-O-Doune, early 1900s. The men were brothers and fellow mine-workers. In those not so far off days, cycling was the in thing and after long hours spent underground it was something of a luxury to saddle up on the bike with a jeely piece and tin flask of cool water. Distance was no object to these men – my father cycled from Kilsyth to Kinloch Rannoch on many occasions.

Duntreath Terrace, on the north bank of the Garrell Burn near Burngreen Park. The iron railing kept the public from the burn, which can rise into a raging torrent after a few hours of heavy rain at any time of year. Fifty yards to the left the Garrell meets the Ebroch Burn, both of which join the River Kelvin after their short journey through the town. The terrace was named after Sir Archibald Edmonstone of Duntreath, who bought the Kilsyth estates for £41,000 in 1782. Duntreath Terrace has, over the years, been upgraded and the desirable properties are handy for Main Street. The decorations were for the coronation of King George VI.

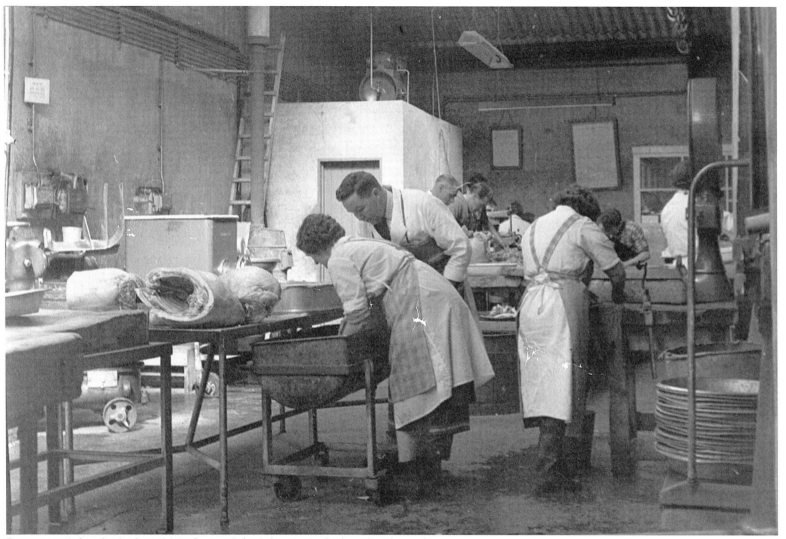

Barrowman's butcher's shop, Main Street. I don't know much about butchers' shops but Barrowman's was considered to be one of the best in town. There were once four butchers' in the town and an abattoir on the banks of the Garrell Burn at the lower end of Backbrae Street.

The name Lockhart was synonymous with one of the finest baker's shops in Kilsyth. This van replaced a horse-drawn model and had just been delivered when the picture was taken. The Lockharts were greatly respected and when times were hard, especially during the strikes, old Mr Lockhart made bread available which families in need could pay for at a later date. The bakery premises were situated on the east side of Main Street.

The Burngreen was used by Lord Livingston and his successors for exercising their horses. It is believed that there was once a monastery in this area, situated between the Garrell and Ebroch Burns. During the Napoleonic Wars, Scotland's senior regiments recruited among the Kilsyth weavers. The Scots Greys horsemen would charge along the green demonstrating their great skill with lances and sabres as they skirmished through the lines of spectators plucking apples from the outstretched hands of the public. At the outbreak of the First World War, the local company of the 7th Battalion Argyll and Sutherland Highlanders left from the small building on the extreme left edge of the picture. The building was Kilsyth school.